A GRATITUDE JOURNAL

for Artists, List-Makers, and Doodlers

Patti Bowman

Silver Linden Press
Salem, Oregon

Published by Silver Linden Press in 2019
First edition; First printing

Illustrations, design and writing © 2019 Patti Bowman
Cover art by Patti Bowman
Cover design by Susan D. Johnson
Special thanks to Bobbi Bowman and Robert Fox for their suggestions and feedback.

ISBN 978-0-9981354-6-5

Dedicated to

Karen

Dear Diane,
I am so grateful for
our friendship!
Love,
Patti

Ideas on how to use this Gratitude Journal:

- Consider using colored pens.

- Experiment with both lined and blank pages.

- FEEL the gratitude as you write, doodle, and draw.

- List 5 or more things you are grateful for. Design a frame around your list.

- Try colored pencils, or drawing pencils.

- Try crayons.

- If something special comes up, write more details about it.

- Explore with markers. Check first to see if they bleed.

- Date your entries.

- Play with emojis.

- Send appreciation to someone who is bothering you.

- Scribble or draw wherever your imagination leads you.

- Send appreciation to your body.

- Become quiet inside and ask Spirit (Divine, Universe) for guidance.

- Write the guidance you receive from Spirit.

- Have fun while you connect with your heart.

- Put your personality into this journal to make it your own.

14

114

About the Author

Patti Bowman is a Certified Nutritionist as well as an Author. Her book, *52 Ways to Transform Your Health One Step at a Time*. includes a section on the importance of gratitude in our lives. Patti understands health is about the whole person. That means having fun, learning, and being creative is included in the whole health picture.

Patti now lives in Salem, Oregon. When she is not cooking healthy food, writing creative books for children. or creating journals, she has fun playing with art supplies. You can learn more about Patti's work here: www.authorpattibowman.com.

Thank you!

Thank you for purchasing this journal! I hope you have found it helpful.
Please share your enthusiasm on Facebook , Twitter, and other social media.

I would also appreciate it if you would leave a short review of the book
online. It will help other people know if this journal is for them. Reviews
also help me improve this and future books.

Much gratitude,
Patti

Other Books by the Author

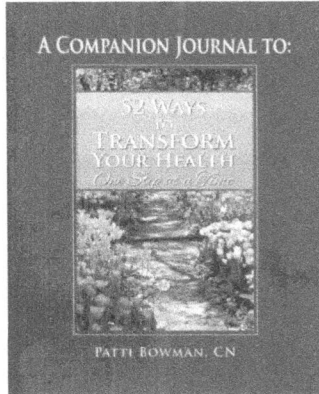

Look for these creative books for children:

journaling giraffes series

A drawing, coloring, writing journal for Kids

Jeremiah Giraffe Explores Art

Patti Bowman

journaling giraffes series

A drawing, coloring, writing journal for Kids

Jonathan Giraffe Visits a Pumpkin Farm

Patti Bowman

journaling giraffes series

A drawing, coloring, writing journal for Kids

Jenny Giraffe Visits the Beach

Patti Bowman

journaling giraffes series

A drawing, coloring, writing journal for Kids

Joshua Giraffe Goes Camping

Patti Bowman

Visit: https://www.journalinggiraffes.com

CPSIA information can be obtained
at www.ICGtesting.com
Printed in the USA
FSHW021044031019
62558FS

9 780998 135465